Getting Rid of That Babypreneur Mentality

It's Time to GROW UP!

Tammie T. Polk

Copyright © 2017 Tammie T. Polk/ Tammie Terrell
Mompreneur Coaching

All rights reserved.

ISBN-13: 978-1979832502

ISBN-10: 1979832501

Welcome to the Challenge! I hope you're ready because we're about to turn both you and your business on its head, but in a good way!

My name is Tammie and I am YOUR Virtuous Business Woman Motivational Makeover Mentor. It is my job to unleash the remarkable business woman within to help you become a woman of lasting influence! I want to see you Rise above your frustration, Reclaim your life and talents, and Evolve into the woman who is free to transform those talents into a treasure—a business all while maintaining a strong family base and your sanity—NOW!

Babypreneur Mentality: Day One--
Do you have
a Babypreneur Mentality?

I did! When I started my business, I depended heavily on others and didn't like when they tried to push me to do more or better. (Think about how babies act when you start giving them tummy time!) The problem was on my end -- I still wanted them to do for me and they wanted me to learn to stand on my own.

Once I did, I became a people pleaser. Like a baby, I showed what I could do and needed constant praise. When I didn't get it, it was a problem for me! However, the more confident I became in my abilities, the more I tried on my own, the more I practiced and honed my craft, the better I got at it. I started being proud of MYSELF!

People didn't like that. They wished for the days where I came to and needed them for everything. When I raised my prices, I lost people. It was because they thought I was doing the most -- they still saw me as a baby. It was hard for them to believe I'd grown up.

It's time to break the Babypreneur Mentality! You're MUCH more valuable than that!

GROW UP!

It's okay to have business besties, mentors and coaches, but one thing you are going to have to do is learn to stand on your own! Validation seeking will kill your business before it even starts. Yes, it's natural for us to want people to love us and what we do, but we have be okay with going forward anyway!

Here are some tips to help you **GROW UP**:

- Do what you can yourself!

People are more likely to help when they know you are trying as opposed to asking them to do it for you right out of the gate.
- Realize that their time is just as valuable as yours! They showed you what to do so that you could go on from there.
- Learn to be your own reward. Figure out what motivates you and use that to spring forward.
- Resist the urge to have baby prices! Stand by the prices that you set, too!

Babypreneur Mentality: Day Two

Babies are not careful at all and often learn the hard way about things. No matter how many warnings they get, they still want to try... and then they get hurt.

What's my point? Do your homework on anyone you want to work with or any innovative approach you may want to try. If everything you see and hear is negative, that might be a sign. While you'll hope that things will be different for you, it may not be the case. As parents hate to see their baby get hurt, those who support and try to help you hate seeing it as well!

GROW UP!

Shiny Object Syndrome will mess you up as a business owner! As your parents may have told you growing up—not everything that's good to you is good for you. Make sure that it will move your business in the right direction before you commit to it.

Here are some tips to help you **GROW UP**:

- Read all reviews and testimonials before even starting a free trial.
- Ask yourself what makes what you see better than what you already have.
- Ask yourself if investing in what you see is going to put your business in an unreasonable or unnecessary amount of debt.
- If it is a person you want to work with, don't be afraid to ask for references, both positive and negative. If they are unwilling to give you those who didn't work out, walk away!

Babypreneur Mentality: Day Three

When a baby is learning to walk, they fall a billion times, but they realize they have a choice to make. They can sit there and cry while waiting for someone to pick them up. They roll over and start crawling because that sometimes works just as well as walking. They get up, try again, fall some more, repeat.

My challenge for you today is the latter. You're building and things are happening. You've fallen, but it's okay! Get up, try again, fall more, and repeat. Why? Think about what happens when a baby gets a handle on walking -- they start to run, their confidence is boosted, they're happy and hard to handle! Just a thought!

GROW UP!

The hardest thing for a business owner to deal with is learning that results aren't always immediate. Another is that failure really isn't failure—it's another opportunity to try something new. A third is that the last letter in the word "No" is the first letter in the word "Opportunity." Things are going to happen and nothing worth having is easy to get.

Here are some tips to help you **GROW UP**:

- Look at what didn't work and ask yourself who, what, when, where, why, how, and how much it is going to take to make it right.
- Ask for help! If you fell because you're trying to do everything by yourself, it's time to build a team to help you.
- No matter what happens, do NOT start beating yourself up nor your business down!
- Don't blame shift. At the end of the day, it all comes back to you. Take ownership of what happened and act accordingly.

Babypreneur Mentality: Day Four

Babies everyday get to the point where they want what others have and will do just about anything to get it! They look at what they have, see that it's different, look at what someone else has, compared it to theirs, put theirs down, and try to take what the other person has. And then, it happens. They get it and it doesn't work for them. They can't make it do what the other baby did.

My point? Comparison! I'm struggling with this element right now. We develop our programs, products, and packages -- and then we are what someone else is doing and start to look down on what we ourselves created. We change ours to make it look like theirs and we're happy about it -- until it takes us in a direction that we don't like. What happens? We go back to what we had and do what we can to make it better.

What you've created is good enough! You know what your target market needs! You know what you want to say and do, how you want it said and done, and when you want to say it and do it. Think about it.

GROW UP!

Nothing about your business has to look anything like what is already out there! Just because you see someone who does what you do, that doesn't mean that they do what YOU do. What you have is different no matter how similar it seems. Do go changing trying to please people when you have raving fans who love you as you are. There's a big difference between stepping your game up and trying to keep up with those you aren't even meant to follow!

Here are some tips to help you **GROW UP**:

- Realize that you have something rare and precious to offer even in the wake of competition, be it real or perceived.

- If you have doubts based on what you see, evaluate what you already have before you go changing things. As the saying goes, if it ain't broke….
- Realize that you won't be everybody's cup of tea and be okay with that.
- Recognize your strong suits and what makes you different from the person you are comparing yourself to. I promise you will see why you don't need to copy them!

Babypreneur Mentality: 5 Day Challenge

Your mission, if you choose to accept it, is to pick one of the area to work on. Here are some questions I want you to ask yourself:

1. How is being a Babypreneur in this area hurting my life and business?
2. Am I still taking baby steps here?
3. What do I need to do in order to help me to "grow up" in this area?
4. What will happen if I don't grow up in this area?

Babypreneur Mentality: Day Six

Baby food...yeah. They always say to start with the veggies first because, if you don't, them a baby will only want the sweet stuff! So, you introduce the veggies and then the fruits. After that, you start giving both. The baby is used to both due to increased expose to them.

As entrepreneurs, we focus on the successes, the fun stuff, the stuff that doesn't take a whole lot of effort, and the easy parts -- if there are any! We sometimes dread the work that goes into getting to that point. We sometimes just don't want to do it! Then, we get mad because we've waited until the last minute to get those laborious tasks done and doing get those same results!

My challenge to you today will be -- forgive the babyish analogy -- to eat your veggies! The fruit will taste a lot better when you do!

GROW UP!

One thing that I have always been annoyed by is coaches who put the fruit our first. While it is necessary to do things to attract people to you, they need those veggies! They want to know the real story, whether you want to tell it or not. They want to know what you failed at, what went wrong, who and what you don't recommend and why – all of that! Don't worry about those who walk away when you put that out there because that will let you know who you're not meant to work with.

Here are some tips to help you **GROW UP**:

- Be transparent and authentic! People need to know you are human.
- Get rid of the fluff in your presentation. People what to know exactly who, what, when, where, why, how and how much so that they can take action immediately.

- Don't make promises or claims that aren't true! It's okay to not know and say so. It works out better when you are up front about that.
- Don't waste people's time. Get to the point! Too much sugar can be a turn off to those listening to you!

Babypreneur Mentality: Day Seven

Babies are fascinated by what they see in the mirror. It takes them a minute to realize that they are looking at themselves. They think it's a completely different person! And then, they realize that it IS them in the mirror and they are excited about it -- so excited that it's hard to get them away from the mirror.

You are beautiful, entrepreneur, but it's time to get out of the mirror and get to work! We miss out on so much because we're too busy looking in the mirror, whether we like what we see or not. When you spend too much time getting ready, time passes you by! So, who's getting out of the mirror today?

GROW UP!

It's all about progress and not perfection! If you wait until everything you lay your hand to is absolutely perfect before you share it with the world, you will lose and annoy people, especially if they've been waiting for any length of time. It's better to put it out there, get feedback, and revamp it later than to wait until it's all fine tuned. You will miss out on your time to shine doing that!

One thing that will keep you down is not starting before you are ready. Build while you are going forward!

Here are some tips to help you **GROW UP**:

- Be honest and ask yourself what will happen if you continue to wait on putting out what's in you.
- Release one part of what you're doing at a time. Doing that will drive more interest your way.
- Know and understand that you won't please everyone.
- Someone somewhere sometime somehow will need that something that you do. If you don't put it out there, they

won't get it!

Babypreneur Mentality: Day Eight

Nothing, to me, is funnier than a sleepy baby! They don't know whether to sleep or cry. They're sleepy, but they don't want to sleep because they think they will miss something. They cry because they're tired. Soon, sleep wins because crying makes them sleepy!

What does this mean for you? Know when it's time to rest. If you're working on something and you have anvils hanging from your eyelashes, it's time to stop. Just a thought!

GROW UP!

If you don't take care of yourself, you won't be any good to anyone! I know how it is—you want to be there and be present for everyone, yet you have to realize that you need to rest and recharge or you won't be!

Here are some tips to help you **GROW UP**:

- Automate as much as you can!

This is one that I am learning myself. The more you can take your hands off of, the more you can get done.

- Realize when it is time to pull back, take a break, and rest. Prepare as much in advance as you can, so that when that time comes, you can walk away without checking on things every 16 seconds.
- Learn to let those who want to help to do so!
- Resist the urge to be in control of everything.

Babypreneur Mentality: Day Nine

Babies have growing pains. Teething, growth spurts, falls, and sicknesses that come from them -- just to name a few. Even though it appears they are going to last forever, soon a baby realizes what they can do once they have those teeth, are a little taller, and can walk or run without falling! Once they figure all that out, Game On!

It's the same for you, entrepreneur! Those painful business tasks -- ads, blog posts, website revamps, overwhelming responses -- must be done and dealt with. Lean business seasons are going to come, but it's all about how you've prepared for them, how you handle them, what you do while you wait, and how hard you come out swinging once it's over! Think about it.

GROW UP!

A friend once told me that trusting our fates to people's humanity will fail us every time! That's why it is important to have your hands on more than one thing so that you can keep going in those lean times. You may have to work for a while to save your business or even collaborate with a competitor in order to get what you need!

Here are some tips to help you **GROW UP**:

- Make a list of 25 things that you are awesome at and can make money from and then break that list down by the time it takes for you to make money from those things. Keep those quick ones in your pocket.
- Have a business rainy day fund to help in those lean times!
- Put together a live or online event – anything that will bring people to you.
- Resist the urge to shut down just

because you hit a lean season.

Babypreneur Mentality: 10 Day Challenge

Your mission, if you choose to accept it, is to pick one of the area to work on. Here are some questions I want you to ask yourself:

1. How is being a Babypreneur in this area hurting my life and business?
2. Am I still taking baby steps here?
3. What do I need to do in order to help me to "grow up" in this area?
4. What will happen if I don't grow up in this area?

Babypreneur Mentality: Day Eleven

Babies think that whatever they have will always be there. When they can't find it, can't use it, or it's broken, they don't know what to do. They can't and won't be satisfied with anything else. They want what they've always had and don't understand why it's not there for them anymore. And, it takes forever for them to get over it. (Oh, and don't them see another baby with one!)

That last part was just for laughs, but I'm talking about technology. While this is a technology driven world, we as entrepreneurs still need to appeal to those who aren't technology users. Yes, they still exist! If everything technological that you have was no longer available to you, how would you run and market your business? How are you reaching those who still want things in their hands and in their mailbox, phone calls, and face to face conversations? Think about it!

GROW UP!

Maintaining an offline presence is just as important as maintaining your online presence. There are still people who want a business card, flyer, or even a phone call! I know it sounds crazy, yet there are still people who don't even have cell phones.

Here are some tips to help you **GROW UP**:

- Have advertising in your local paper and other relevant print publications in your advertising budget.
- Realize that flyers and business cards are still the way to go in some cases.
- Update printed promotional pieces regularly and don't keep a lot on hand.
- Resist the urge to walk away

from someone who asks you to do things the old-fashioned way. You might be missing out on money!

Babypreneur Mentality: Day Twelve

When a baby is feeling bad, they are miserable! They don't want to eat. They don't want to play. All they want to do is sleep and be cuddled. Everything stops!

We are the same way. When we are not feeling our best, we try to push through knowing good and well that we aren't going to get anything done. Take care of yourself first!

GROW UP!

I'm going to keep it simple. Be aware of what you eat, read, listen to, and watch as well as who you hang around. Any hiccups in these areas will torpedo everything you endeavor to do.

Here are some tips to help you **GROW UP**:

- If something doesn't feel right, go to the doctor or other medical professional! Suffering in silence makes things worse.

- Identify what not so great habits you need to change.
- If it doesn't inspire, encourage, uplift, or equip you to move forward, let it go!
- Resist the urge to say that you're okay. Your body will prove you wrong every time!

Babypreneur Mentality: Day Thirteen

When a baby sees something on the floor, what's the first thing they do? They pick it up and put it in their mouths. It doesn't matter what it is--it's headed straight for their mouths. They must be taught what is okay to put in their mouths and what isn't!

It's the same way with entrepreneurs. We see something new and we feel like we must have it. We must get involved. We don't understand those who are telling us that it's not a good idea. We keep looking at it. We want it and we don't care what the cost is. Sometimes, that's the quickest way to get burned!

Every webinar you see isn't meant for you to watch. Every coach you see isn't meant for you to work with. Every strategy session or clarity call means that you should work with that person. Every new approach isn't meant for you to try. There are times when staying in your safety zone is best! Think about it...

GROW UP!

I'm going to mention Shiny Object Syndrome again here. Shiny Object Syndrome is like going to the grocery store hungry—you end up spending way more than you want to, buying things you don't need and can't return, and wasting food because you bought something that doesn't taste as good as you thought it would. The same thing can happen in business!

Here are some tips to help you **GROW UP**:

- Question yourself! Do you really need it? Is your business going to fall apart if you don't do or have it?
- Consider the source of information you are given about something and weigh it against the scope of your business.
- Be willing to listen to those who

are trying to keep you from doing it. They may be right!
- Resist the urge to do it anyway! You could be headed for disaster.

Babypreneur Mentality: Day Fourteen

Think about a time when you've seen a baby go into spaghetti mode. The adult they're with is practically dragging them because they're trying to get them to do something they don't want to do. They feel like if they go into spaghetti mode that they'll be left alone. Nope! That adult ignores the whining and pushes them forward. Eventually, they do it.

This was me a few months ago. I went into spaghetti mode. What I was being encouraged to do needed to be done. It had to be dragged out of me! However, after I did it, I started to understand why it needed to be done.

Whatever you're being dragged to do, get it done. You'll come to understand why a LOT sooner than you think!

GROW UP!

No matter how tedious your daily tasks may seem, they still need to get done. Going spaghetti mode will only lead to you regretting that you didn't get it done when you had the chance! You will find yourself further behind and working your way back up can be harder than getting things done on the front end.

Here are some tips to help you **GROW UP**:

- Think about what will happen if you let spaghetti mode have its way.
- If you have a long list, choose five things that you can get done in an hour's time.
- Don't try to do a million things at one time. Stretch large projects out over time.
- Resist the urge to pay someone to do it for you out of laziness! You'll end up fixing their mistakes.

Babypreneur Mentality: Day Fifteen

    A baby that already knows how to do something but still wants it to be done for them is frustrating! Why? It's because, when they are caught doing it for themselves, it makes the person that did that for them mad! Think about it! You've carried that baby around, thinking they couldn't walk yet. Then, you catch them walking on their own! When they get caught, they immediately sit down and hold their arms out to be picked up. What do you do? You say, "Oh, no! I'm not picking you up ANYMORE. You gone have to walk from now on. You should've never let me see that!"

    What I'm about to say is going to strike a nerve and, for that, I apologize! Yes, as entrepreneurs, we will need carrying every now and then. Yes, as entrepreneurs, we may find ourselves depending on a trusted someone to help get us over our hurdles, and that's okay!

The problem comes in when we've learned and know how to do better, but still let that person kill themselves trying to make it happen! And the day that they see that we can do what they did and produce the same results, all while they were going full throttle -- WATCH OUT!

GROW UP!

Quit acting like you don't know what to do because that crutch is gone out from under you! You aren't going to die because their time in your life and business is done. Getting mad because you have to run your business isn't going to cut it.

Here are some tips to help you **GROW UP**:

- Realize that YOU have to run your business and that means doing things yourself when it's neccssary.
- Realize that their time is just as valuable as yours! They showed you what to do so that you

could go on from there.
- Learn to stand on your own once you have gotten a handle on what you were shown.
- Resist the urge to beg them to stick around! They have goals and a business of their own to run!

Babypreneur Mentality: 15 Day Challenge

Your mission, if you choose to accept it, is to pick one of the area to work on. Here are some questions I want you to ask yourself:

1. How is being a Babypreneur in this area hurting my life and business?
2. Am I still taking baby steps here?
3. What do I need to do in order to help me to "grow up" in this area?
4. What will happen if I don't grow up in this area?

Babypreneur Mentality: The End

You made it through the challenge! How do you feel? Great, I hope! My goal during this challenge was to help you to look at your business in a childlike manner so that you could make the hard decisions that you need to make. Having a childlike view of your business can serve you in ways you may have never thought or and that's a good thing!

Now that you've finished, purpose to move forward because your business and those that you serve are expecting you to do just that!

If you need to hop on a call, reach out and let me know. Until next challenge, BREAK THAT BABYPRENEUR MENTALITY!

www.ingramcontent.com/pod-product-compliance
Lightning Source LLC
Chambersburg PA
CBHW040250220526
45473CB00001B/439